Thread of Fire

Poems of Peril, Longing, and Loss

Nancy Brady Cunningham

Riverhaven Books

www.RiverhavenBooks.com

Thread of Fire is a work of the author's creation.

Published in the United States by Riverhaven Books,
www.RiverhavenBooks.com

ISBN : 978-1-937588-87-8

Printed in the United States of America

Edited and designed by
Stephanie Lynn Blackman
Whitman, MA

Cover Photo Credit: Nancy Brady Cunningham

Dedication

To Dolores
my friend and mentor,
and the impetus behind this book

Acknowledgements

My warm thanks to my mentors Ricky Riccio, Tom Daley, and Dolores Stewart Riccio for their friendship, encouragement, and critiques. I am also grateful to the poets in Dolores' online and in-person groups for their honest assessment of my work.

Off the Coast: Summer 2008, Vol.XIV, Number 2:
Overwinter

black bough: a journal of haiku and related poetry:
issue #11:
fresh grave

New England Greater Brockton Society for Poetry and the Arts Poetry Contest 2010:
Rising (a finalist)

TABLE OF CONTENTS

Peril

Friday Night Ride

she dropped her husband
by the tavern door
drove forward
to the undertakers
offering her goodbye
to a younger woman –
a friend who woke no more

she passed at night
a June night like this one
coming on soft and full
holding another daybreak
as the forsaken promise
impossible to keep

within the hour
back at the bar –
night swallows
her black Toyota
the pub packed –
parking scarce
she drives a whole block
beyond where that
glass of chill white waits

she sees three open spaces
lined up along the curb
pulls into the spot
closest to the bar

puts it in park
unclicks the belt
pops the lock
window beside her fills
a form too close
inches beyond the glass

silent circling
of his index finger
roll it down

their eyes meet
she keeps hers blank
he unbuttons his shirt
points at his belt

ain't got no gun no knife
sudden breeze
flutters his shirt

faster now
his finger
same gesture

key still on –
she turns away
slips her hands
to the wheel of fortune

glides forward
straight through
the two empty spaces –
gray meters stand sentry

she hooks a right
and drives
like a one-eyed
queen of clubs
leaving Satan
way behind

Afternoon Nap

a hooded being
short of stature
transparent as dusk
stares while I sleep

a raucous ring –
I startle awake
glimpse the dark-eyed form
standing beside my couch

in mid-lunge
bolting toward the phone
I slam one leg
through this dim figure

gone
like meadow mist
in a burning sun –
vanished

was it a harbinger
        a loved one's ghost
        a warning

or did it come for me

Out on the Town

highbeams slash thick woods
car snakes endless curves –
a shortcut to Providence

two young women
dressed in cleavage and short skirts
slide through the stop sign   turn left

giddy excitement shapes
loud chatter of bands and drinks –
June heat lingers in dark creases

flickering faces appear –
a knot of men stand outside
the local rod and gun

intent eyes pierce the women
deep voices   guttural sounds
penetrate the interior

car slides past   night hides them
one woman grabs her sweater
fending off the chill

driver rolls her window shut –
closes them in stench of sweat
trickling down scented bodies

King Tide

unyielding water
pushes over
a narrow strip
of barrier sand
onto eel-grass bed
meant to slow it

seawall only intensifies
the fury –
ever larger waves
batter the stone barricade
pounding it under

storm surge moves
onto higher ground
driving waves
into dry places

nothing blunts
the violence –
a cottage drops
from the bluff
into the sea

Fire Bearer

For Michael "Wolf" Pasakarnis
(June 25,1981- September 8, 2010)

a young man strides up Burial Hill
to bear witness to
old grounds
old graves
old growth trees
the huge beech at the crest
calls him to sit a while
close his eyes
drift toward reverie

it is the fall of the year
when summer swelter
gives way to autumn cool
in the belly of a cloud –
the young man remains lost
in vivid imagery –
unaware of the clash
of water and dust
of heat and cold

a single jagged knife carves
a channel through electric air
a hissing invades his body –
like a fire-eater at the circus
he ingests the blinding white
all shadows disappear

the tree unscathed lives on –
the young man never leaves

Look Out

"Pisgah" in Hebrew means *lookout* or *place with a view.*

we climb the long gravel road
to the summit of Mount Pisgah
then clamber up wooden stairs

seven flights to the fire tower
that crowns this small mountain –
lakes and forests shimmering below

beckon us this August morning
we strike out against routine
we forego retracing the road

we plunge into thick woods
start down the steep backside of Pisgah
looking for blue paint on tree trunks –

symbols for the Blueberry Trail
that leads round to the lot
where our cars wait

though we find no blue-marked trees
the slope at last flattens out
we stumble onto a trail   *must be the Blueberry*

beguiled by thick pine scent
by sun-spangled forest floor
by mushrooms in a dozen shades

Judi and I sink into the magic
of our walk in the wilderness
we never glance back

never observe the shape of boulders
never notice when the path widens
never ponder the lack of hikers

we come upon crude signs
where hand-painted arrows
point toward distant towns

we're lost in the wrong season –
our wild hearts have blundered
onto a snowmobile trail

we backtrack and switch paths
unaware of the circle we're forming
till Pisgah seems to rise from its center

we begin the steep sweaty climb
up the mountainside   breath heaving
we reach the top and discover

no fire tower
no access road
no view

thick canopy obscures
all chance of orientation
we've fallen off the map

if only we could fly west
hold fast to afternoon light
arrive home before dark...

we dial *emergency* –
in the elasticity of time
we stretch toward rescue

Playing the Horses: First Encounter

back door closes and closes
March wind blusters against asphalt
he keeps his motor running
at the edge of the Heights

she spots his powder blue Ford –
continental kit shining
on lowered rear chassis –
he leans across   pushes door wide

she slides into Heartbreak Hotel
smoldering from the dash
noboysnocarsnotrack
beats a counter-rhythm in her mind

at the red light she slouches down –
a gaggle of girls from her grade
keeps within crosswalk lines
straight as the nuns at St. Theresa's

he's off to slap twenty on a hot one –
shouldering into the shiftless crush
waving greasy bills   yelling at
the cigar-chewing cashier

her sideways glances search for
wavy brimmed hats   paisley ascots
jubilant roses strung together
in a necklace   winner take all

Playing the Horses: First Encounter   Page 2.

afternoon light diminishes –
racing forms litter the ground
he peels out onto route one
exhausting her MGM dreams

Project looms   redbrick sameness
glowering in a setting sun
again he parks on the outskirts –
scent of Aqua Velva closes in

lips skim hers   heat lightning
flashes beneath flared skirt –
her insides twist this way only
when she sits close to Paladin

his Friday-night kisses blazing
through the black-and-white TV
touching her secret place where
smell of bloodfear now mingles

with steamy car windows –
no *havegunwilltravel* here
only one hand reaching for
the cold metal handle

he murmurs *stay* tugs at her coat –
his sweet hurricane kisses
press against *supperdarkhome*
she leans away   door opens out

she takes the slow long road
she burns through the icy wind

Riptide Afternoon

for Devin

the way gravity attracts
all bodies toward the center
an August swelter drew
the family to Goosewing

his wife and children slept
like folded towels on a blanket
the girl blond to match the sand
the boy's eyes green as seaglass

the man grabs his boogie board
ploughs into shallow water
ocean swells tempt him deeper
until a rogue wave dumps him

he focuses salt-stung eyes
in time to see his *Wave Rider*
caught in the belly of a roller
washing toward shore

he clips his panic
attempts to keep parallel
while a giant vacuum
drags him out to sea

waves swamp him a second time
he tires   tries treading
onshore his wife shields her eyes
sees his board sloshing at her feet

he spots a surfer paddling nearby
ready to climb his surfboard
the man burns through the blueblack
of the sea to his voice   hollers

wind snares his words
waves slice away meaning
the surfer begins to board
then casually turns

did you say something?
the man in animal exhaustion
gestures for help
surfer paddles toward him

sees the man's eyes   offers his board
and swims beside the prostrate form
all the way to waist-high water
the man sloshes in   staggers up the beach

he collapses on a tiny square of refuge
sinking now into warm sand and their embraces
they lie there till the sun slides behind dunes
time to go home

that night over and over
he drifts off   slips beneath
the gasp of seawater lungs
can't touch bottom

he panics   eyes swim open
his stare sees only
the underside of waves –
all air an attic away

Il Duomo, Firenze, Italy
for Cara

Michelangelo dragged blocked angels
through these streets
Dante sang as he sauntered down
this narrow passage

church bells toll against autumn blue
my daughter and I rush toward the train
hurry! hurry! we'll miss it

we dash through the center
crushed   crowded   swept along
dog droppings on pavement
blunt stares of men
drench of garlic on someone's breath
glancing blows of
closed umbrellas   black-clad elbows   Gucci bags
turn at the next corner!

there she is
breathing calm
hovering
in terracotta   pale green   and vanilla
her head huge
her limbs reaching for us
the mother
often invisible
ever present
murmuring
you are provided for

Rising

she takes her hand as they cross
chooses the flowers
they pick at the market
forbids even ear piercing

daughter shrinks from her
slow heavy step while flowers
weigh down the swinging hips
of almost thirteen

he watches her
skinny legs long
to skip over
the edge of the world

in a black shiny limo
snorting horsepower
he glides up the dirt road
sipping a pomegranate
cosmopolitan in the back seat
he lowers tinted glass
offers her a sip
*won't you come in
out of the glare?*
his gold chains
outshine the sun

shrugging out of a shiver
Persephone slides into cool
dark-leather seats
sinking deeply
his ashen fingers
leave their impression
on her bare thigh

Longing

Overwinter

Homage to Homero Aridjis

don't let me go
like a faded meadow tossed to an early snow
and don't let me go
like the last monarch drifting southward
and when small clumps of Mexican firs
summon orange wings
veined in black and edged in white spots
don't let me be one with the quivering clusters
beating above the backbone of the Appalachians
don't let me go

my flagging limbs signal you again
while I reach for the trees
atop mountain ridges near El Rosario
your voice dies away
crossing the gray breath of my wings
shivering toward sanctuary

Night Blooming Cereus

for Denise Geddes

prefers the dark
warm and moist
the tree-like plant
pulls you
toward its swirl –
closed petals
pale flesh

tight patterns undulate
the perfume anoints your body
scent of whispered secrets
unfolding

each languid petal
drapes radiance
over islands of night air

this shapeshifter
opens only
at your blackest hour –
a harbinger offering
but one chance

take the risk –
this unsettling beauty
dies into the garish light

Hymn to Gaia

take us in
we've thrown our light about
craving edgelessness
in the wider meadow

take us in
corn husked into forgiven
we dreamt ourselves
dwelling inside

take us in
you breathed us
deep as field furrows
in a pasture of seed

we endured
our clipped hair
our ruined faces

we hear your voice
and wait:
such things take time

but the prairie train is leaving
and the orchard spills its prophecy
from unspooled lower branches

while we pine for you
the friend
take us in

Provincetown

April on the outer cape
a sacrament of cleansing
the rain-washed light
smells like mercy

To My Brother in His Forgetfulness
for Brady

you walk alone into the Hansel forest
birds are eating your memory crumbs
your life's rung out in dull clangs
the hours leaking into a devoured mind

last night I dreamt us young –
third-floor door locked against
dry dust smell of tenement stairs
the unpainted kitchen
bent beneath its muted gray
where empty stove pans
coated your tongue with a color
that tastes of cheap aluminum

this morning brings crow-black wings
relentless in their noiseless flapping –
your eyes push against me like a plea
to bear in mind the fairytale and
Gretel unlocking the cage door

January is Named for Janus
for June

it doesn't matter
that he wears two faces
back to back

that he looks east
to days that never
will rise again

that he looks west
to the burning descent
of your days

that you look
in both directions
till the two become one

that there was
a passage out
you couldn't find

that the doorway
to the guest room
stands ajar

at your sister's house
where you slept
then woke to Janus

slipping the gray dawn
of your hair through
fingers of moon

April
for Meredith

garden gates open
winter whimpers away

your lungs linger on
psalms of welcome

your voice sings
the burgeoning light

Woodland Walk

only you
bend to loosen
hunched snow
liberating
burdened boughs

my stooped shoulders
lighten

Loss

The Closing
for Ed

this morning a stranger
took possession of
our lakeside cabin
dwarfed by stately pines

yesterday I was a siren
among wild tree spirits
today I shrink from
sun on bare breasts

my body never will again
bend to that earthen patch –
a divining rod once drawn
to deeper wellsprings

I slide my face
behind the mask –
a dealer content
to trade the land

for silver dollars –
the ink dries
the coins clink
where is the joy?

To a Friend Showering

you wipe away the gloss
and the blush
lean your spine into
an evaporated spray

your nightshirt hangs
on a porcelain hook
one breast pocket stitched
one not

flakes of glitter polish
cling to your nails
you pull aside
the plastic curtain

blurt of grafted skin
framed in the mirror
I watch you clutch
at a frayed towel

Quitting Time

with dad gone
we run from our life
in the projects

mom herds us
up three flights
into a tenement crawlspace
beneath unfamiliar eaves

a pale evening sun
slips through the blinds –
patterns of dull grease
stripe the kitchen wall

a horn blast rises
from the curdled air below –
the mill's letting out

we stand at the open window
stare down at a street
filled with strangers

someone's waving goodbye

Mourning

they buried your body
but what remains
visits me still –

a stab of inspiration
an ache of scattered words
a stain of beauty

you glide close
insistent through the fog –
I long to follow

like a sheared lamb

Grieving – The Second Year

flowers choked your coffin
it's early spring   you've left me
bound to winter

barefoot in snowdrifts
my body a wind-shook tree
I watch hundreds of days vanish

dishes and dusting intrude
on our intimate chats –
twelve months you were the one

passenger in my car –
my only companion when
the shower unleashed its tears

the garage needs cleaning –
a cold slap against
the cheek of reverie

my heart's
out of rhythm
how can I revive you

I crave the ragged fog
the haunted memories –
I enter a wilderness

where the mundane
ambushes my mind
forces me into neglect

I'm greedy for grief
and all its unknowns
I'm losing you

Widow

the water
of his gaze
slowed to glass

still hearing
the whirl
of his reel
the hooked fish
dangles

thrown back

As the Crow Flies

she slips through the ribs
roosts in the heart
her feathered shoulders
wrap the mourning close
slow spread of wings
tears a hole in the muscle

her rasp tunnels upward
black bill opens
harsh raucous caw
speaks midnight

she lets loose a broken tirade
that sounds almost human
in an alto voice
that mimics mine
or is

To Lee In Her Dying

how can I utter the first prayer in this new year

why does ocean breathing go unsung in your lungs

what can I offer you to take along
    on the winter-black sea you travel

how will moonlight fall on the soft snow of your face

where are the blinking stars of your eyes visible

why do fallow fields lie trapped in
    the times I failed you

Summerland Roses

for Dolores Sttewart Riccio, d. May 21, 2017

I open the night window
face the empty east
touch flame against wick
scent of oranges
spiked with ginger

this oil of tranquility
speaks the essence
of a peace
I cannot find

the candle's label reads
mountain temple
but on what lost mountain
in which far temple
are you hiding

I am quieter
more interior
does my silence pull you
toward my being

I puff out my chest
inhale deeply
will there be room
in my lungs
for you to breathe again

I press folded hands
over my heart
will you enter –
a rose sipping water
from a thin glass jar

Fresh Grave

in the honking
of the geese
my husband's voice
startles me awake
why is he calling the dog
it's still dark

www.ingramcontent.com/pod-product-compliance
Lightning Source LLC
Chambersburg PA
CBHW022344040426
42449CB00006B/712